THE GLASS EYE

Other books by David Appelbaum

Everyday Spirits (SUNY Press)
An Alchemist at Heart (Codhill Press)
notes on water (Monkfish)
Portuguese Sailor Boy (Eyewear)
Collector of Lapsed Times (Black Spring Publishing Group)

THE
GLASS
EYE

·

David Appelbaum

Epigraph Books
Rhinebeck, New York

ISBN 9781966293095

Contact the publisher for Library of Congress Control Number

Book and cover design by Colin Rolfe
Front cover art: "The Eye, Like a Strange Balloon Moves Towards Infinity" (1882) by Odilon Redon

Epigraph Books
22 East Market Street, Suite 304
Rhinebeck, New York 12572
(845) 876-4861
epigraphpublishing.com

To Kate

As salt, keep your savour,
as light be not obscured.
Charles Olson

Contents

Berthing

CARRY-ONS

Spin-off

There was paralysis in the beginning.

The sea floated dunes
fertile and barren, a world.

It called me twice without voice.

I had no need to ward off anything.
I had no need to console
or disdain.

There were fronds for thatching
under mango trees

smelling of apples or grass.

I threw pebbles into the sky
and cried when they fell.

I labored in the garden
in a utopian smock or shift

while in your hazel eyes
a flash reflected a nearby star.

You minded the children who would stray,
carefree, playing with starfish
washed ashore, abandoned without guilt—
dried like a pit of some fruit.

I remember crab shells and tea chests
that kept moments lost yet preserved:
that was called satori.

Time gathered
hoarded, never spent
then let go like breath taking fright.

My dreams
febrile, sterile,
without continuance

I was a man
I had come to beg,
shaking hairfine rootlets from earth,
dry, moist, used up, unmade

I was human. I ate, I slept
I dreamt of companionship.

I was denied.

To mirror

My sister was in the closet
pretending it was a night club.
A radio downstairs, music
with words smothered by a shroud.
Books lay around, collusion.
Homework: therein lay hope of being
someone when you grew up.

She spied through the keyhole,
choosing morsels past
to feed pride or grievance.
Shouts from the dinner table,
a violin droned an aimless raga.
Mutely, I pounded
a leather mitt with one fist.

In a medieval painting
a mirror in one corner,
you looked at yourself, trapped.
in a flat lozenge.

Whispers of war on TV
antagonized scouring burnt pots.
Odd correspondences.
The spine of her Cervantes book cracked
like a ball against a bat.

At the table, our mother
a dozen errands for nervous hands
passes lamb stew,
salt cellar over-brimming.
a snowfield whitens the tablecloth.

Napkin folds open, reopens
infancy: a moment taught
meant to be outgrown.
To overlook clues
that tell what words really say,
to leave out feelings never fully felt
to be without remorse
when our response went astray.

A bloodline, denial
gave each prayer a place.

Adopted by a home whose
walls we will pound to dust,
collapse into a ragged esplanade
encircling black chaos.

Faded cloth

A shadow, a shimmer
a trace
where one was present to a second.

Some likeness made us.
Before there was
a white candle for a heart,
immortal witness.
There was no love,
looks only, sister, dyed blonde
the mirror has grayed.

Before waking
before dreams, alone in water
unredemptive weight of an incubus,
no earth
only sand-pocked mollusk holes

before brown molecules scatter
before cells replicate form
before fall into being
longing for the upper world
single as we are two

script of my mother
script of my father

you ever restore in me
a trace that
will wake
my sister, analog herself,
look back at me
eyes sparked in festive mirth.

You suffer remembering.
I have lied. I forget.

You ask, what am I here for?

A cell split first light
never alone, always one.

Before dawn your eyes ask,
why us?

Pleasures

Here on earth
on wet meadowgrass,
pressed by night sky, nap blanket,
to mind you,
anxiety, annunciation.

Calm dead air
not yet breathed
by the beauty
that goads my soul to work.

A shirt clings
frozen to my back
rock pillow, broken watch
sleep crab-walks lost
under a milky sea of stars.

The canopy jubilates.
Am I wed?
Strawberry scar on my forehead—
talisman or curse—
draught of coming sorrow.

When dawn breaks
to give strength back,
I squander the harvest of my theft.

Would you give away
 joy that feels itself
a guest who crashed the gate?

Destination

In repetition, comfort
is pain that sees the promise

broken, hope
murdered in a dark well
as stars appear overhead

one by one

a world lit by fire.
You were created
for a damp eon, Pleistocene

willing to evolve in
least solace

young hunger roused
by some quaint deceit
in a life consumed

unlived in a void

spent putting toys
in place for sleep.

The path demurs.

Infirm

In wonder I see eighty years wide.
That man in the mirror
evenly fit to image
nearly (minus time) the same
in the present, eyes squint
to make the lie fit.

He is a recent version, tensed
in success, thinking causally
because thought then was (I told myself)
redaction of feeling.

He was then more passive,
inert, down on being alone (he wasn't)
a boy impatience for years
when there is no need to look ahead.

Other children didn't
which let them be friendly toward him.
He had a glass eye.
He learned a smile,
for parties which he ghosted.

Frozen moments were a plague.
Meek, timid, wishing
to be met, disdaining welcome
because it was banal:
he, trapped in the cell of purity,
practicing deprivation,
sought grace in the tragic
since who suffers sacrifice
of desire gets it back.

You learn insolence
answering without reply
in gestures of proof,
that way, feigning truth.

Falsity, stiffness
assertion by contraries
casts him outside himself
beyond facts to
the hidden: his special role
kept him from the world.

Others remained in the dark
of his absolute need
to efface the mirror—
avowing dimness.

The birthday is past. I feel years
proportion me and also leave
a vacancy I call the possible,
a moment dreaded
for exultation it might bring.
That anguish recalled, the word
I called it, *singularity*.

A trifle

The glass globe was where I wanted to live.
Blunt words of my mother told me
(I presumed) it was impossible.

My wish was childish.
Size forbid it, a body wouldn't fit.
Injury would be the story.
From which I inferred disobedience
that was to change my life.

It was the lesser pain,
watching fake snowflakes whiten
a miniature Niagara Falls,
in fury of each storm
after which the blizzard condensed
into a charmed winter scene.

I grew up watching. In a while
my sister came and sat beside me.
It was not used to housing another soul.
Magically I was doubled—
another mind, another body but just me.

She said we repeat the way we aren't
though you chose to be selfish.
I too (she said) see how each event
needs proof of the truth,
that is, my right to be. I too live
apart from the crowd.

Since my greed was for safety
I played with nonchalance.
Now I (she said) will sit with you.

Now you can't hide any difference.

The guardian

Honesty, a good life, sample hopes
weighed by my guardian angel.
I asked for a place; I learned
to feel homeless.
I asked for peace; I was provided with
strife, struggle and grief
pretending to be someone else.
How did I believe she heard me?

Distractedly, though an ear keened
for slips that parsed clever meanings
as though she was my adversary
and her aim, to teach humility.

Angels, I felt, were masters at words,
Didn't their name mean *messenger*?
My feelings as a boy—hidden,
obverse, disabled—were kneaded,
leavened with the belief
suffering oneself left us
open to others who felt the same,
veterans whose wounds we shared
with tried patience of lovers.

A child's fear made life simple.
A global battle for goodness
about which my daemon would discuss,
retract, or lecture me on language.
Daytime reveries taught how
to point my words, correcting ambivalence.
How precise in voice they grew.

Poignant, assertive, yet clueless.
If I was a neurotic freighted with issues,
it was a madness divine. By night
the moon's phases that philosophers read.
On the earth, *terra lucida*, I sought
enlightened beings who walked in disguise.
I found none.

Fullness of lessons, days heavy
in counsel, nights equally active
save rests between holy words.

I didn't pray.

Language

Lesson of the long view,
never use the word *glad*..
Never mention, never attribute
never believe as a child
one bathed in God's good graces.

Imagination being the exception
to prove the rule,
we could show our faith in fantasies
family picnics or birthday gifts.
Salvation in common pleasures.

This imperative to remain silent:
did one of us lack conviction?
An exam daily given.

You copied teachers' words,
duty to stem one's pleasure.
I improvised in mute hypocrisy
an avenging angel's presence.

We learned an adversarial mind
defining those poor in spirit.
We read elegies praising selfless deeds
divinely punished, with diction
that incited rebellion.

Secret pain revealed like-minded others:
disaffected, statements given to
trail toward martyrdom
sympathy from anyone rejected,
you and I, axis of insurrection
yet never on the same side.

Subtle deep feeling, a talisman,
waked me once at sunrise
to be recognized only in stillness,
it breached everyday life—coffee
drips, birdsong hum, cigarets,
the city off to work—
to address the barrenness
of my ways, the dragon
shadow condensing thought, insomnia.

A breath, ours, hallowed
this gift of transparency.

In the garret

In near paralysis, fall colors
downshift in the stiffening breeze.

A friend's cabin, sloping lawn.
No car, no electric, just woods.
A weekend to meet each other.

Again and again we surrendered
until you cried *potatoes*.

Laughter that angels heard.

We both were soon to ascend,
to jubilate with astral host.
A moon conducted murmurs
from a talk show on the radio.

Words slurred, slow music—
some popular tune—of unhappy love,
a woman betrayed, life in ruins,
relics of joy turned ashen,
a silent scream, banal misery.

The static sounded elegy,
a lamenting soul
in ecstasy of wounds.
What we both undoubtedly underwent.

Neither had the smallest inkling
that we were wrong.

After many meetings,
what alone remains of the night—

a jazzy song that never made
the hit parade.

Hot diggity dog.

Petty crimes

We knew theft of stolen glances,
jigsaw pieces want the puzzle complete.
Always, your eye my life.

Glances charged with imprecise intent
rigid inside of each other's face
registry of feeling, log of travel,
people accounted for, choices delayed,
so separation was like a heat mirage
that hid the fraternal bond
behind shimmering air.
No visible threat but voice hissed
to tie my stomach in knots.

On reflection, purity denied
a permit to accept any reason
for intimacy or love for the other
since difference always exists.

Abhorrence affected me for years,
restraint, our mood, drew me back
to obsessively search my lost identity.
There was none.
Nothing was lost.

Intensity was unendurable.
I believe it made its absence joyful
as if after bed-ridden from ill-health
a simple passion for living
quietened the mind we, in some sense, shared.
An impulse to speak then became normal.

When contact with the world faced
danger in the other's look returned—
that I wanted from fear of exclusion.

Repetition marks a beginning
(effaced) that offers escape
from a place to which I was bound
and bound by my own choosing.

But repetition only repeated
repeatedly.

Strategy

On earth, things count in numbers.
We honor the greater.
Isn't election in God's grace?

My sister doesn't wipe the tears.
Without a word, she crawled under
the dining room table and refused
to go to school.

When you act different you
stand out like eye makeup.
Outside is where they put you.

My sister, grounded, spent days
playing pickup sticks.
After, coming down to eat,

she beamed counting secrets
she'd parse out to our parents.

Our mother, trying to answer, asks
do you win anytime?
She ducks her head
before diving below table-level,
her spilt milk prompts
a repeat (angry) of the question.

Who wins a game of solitaire?

On the beach

There was Calf Pasture, a beach
on the Sound, hemmed by pine trees.

My sister and I were dropped off
with our mother. A red cooler
her mix of grape and pineapple juice.

We had no umbrella. You coated your body
with sand as best you could
or bobbed freezing in salt water
then warmed wrinkled prune skin
then baked red in unforgiving heat.

When I let myself look,
why they called me skinny was obvious.
I wondered if it meant something else.
Like a disease.

My sister had no problems.
A filly, she pranced around
raising sand storms along mad forays.
She stampeded when she was bored.

The ocean made me cower. It wasn't
the real ocean but I didn't know.
One time nearly drowned in an undertow
I learned there was no difference.

Water couldn't be trusted.

The horizon was fascinating
it was there until it opened
letting out a dizzy feeling

that turned me toward families lying about.
Mothers and fathers (a few) had bodies
made mostly of flab and fat,
not how I wanted to look,
like the Lone Ranger or Batman.

I was that as long as my breath was held.

The gaze

Star rise. With sound-effects.
Whoosh of car curbside.
Breath, when it gains height
to be level with the horizon,
trees, hills, brookside where couples gathered
fine, subtle light—
whose blood coursed through dreams
of body warmth,
absolving them of nervous choice,
being reasonable like bankers
and housewives living in big houses
with honey's cloyed monotony.

In the dawn below Ursa Major
lovers, ourselves, lay on fieldgrass.
Patient, you thought not what happens
but the story that tells it
as if bodies were too dense for actuality.

Workday items, business as usual.
People shower and dress, stars
resume their figurations, fade.
The hill is extravagantly marked for trespassing,
giant anthills block every trailhead.

Memory that disjoins image from fact
that reins in being, life on hold:
if I can't recall the night
is it effaced with these words?

Deep down the well, stars are visible.
Looking almost touches the hand of God.

Thales the Greek knew this.
We, you and I, have been gifted proof.

We never believed it.

Love recurs

Turned up blanket. Sun
wakes me after a nightmare one breath before.
morning, glutinous, oozing
present life, acts like a primitive animal.

Yellow apples in a wood bowl.
Radio from a basement room
rain that thrums the windowpane.

Thought lacks substance unlike rain
that floods downstairs without intent.

Last year the same day
another storm prophesied this,

conspiracy makes history,
a plot repeats
machinations between us
fear or impulse. Early morning

ore smelted into memory
banished from earth that bore it.
Thought succumbs to languor
of denial, to make no sense

of tears brimming your eyes
salt with solace, cleansed
of cosmic dust, a chalky gray
rain falls, a screen
against eternal lapping of return.

Risen with hypnotic vision.

Pilgrimage

We each were given a toy valise.
Both had a beige stripe.
Inside, necessaries, different since
we wanted different things.

We lugged them heavily, desires
strange and common, their takes
on truth or errancy or disaster
blurring one with the other.

Earth was yellow with dust
autumn leaves, furrowed anguish
pressed between two panes of glass,
taped cocky with pride and disaffection.
They discolored the kitchen table.

Each leaf single in striving
with that urge peculiar to its species,
to belong, silently, without address,
felt, then erased, again lodged
in the very marrow of our bones.

Urgency, a shadow lengthened
to sunset, remorse gnawed
into *schmutz* of old age when
a sweet smell ought to arise
calming like a new word, *repent*.

In sleep it disturbed dreams.
Nor did day's round soothe it.
Inversely night became a refuge
when desire gave back to ourselves
the real risk of knowing nothing.

Terror of the situation.

War games

My sister collected lady bugs.
She put them in hickory shells
she called boats. They were marked
for a stream that oozed from muck.
It was a river for her. We played
in the swamp while we waited for our lives
to happen. We played war. It was
bugs *versus* newts, a sort of try-out
of being good sports.

Our parents were happy with our rivalry.
(One of many.) We were happy
with lessons of victory and default.

That our lives hadn't occurred yet was obvious.
When they did, my sister had another name.
Playing war was distress of waiting.
We weren't certain what we awaited.

We slogged around damp ground
taking strategic positions, feeling
our bodies change seasonally with the mud
at first taller, then muscle and hair
in unexplored pouches.

And strange impulses, liking to cry.
With a fist, I plowed a deeper trench
for newts, my sister made tiny flags
for boat shells. There were SOS's.

We would tell stories of battles.
There were heroics, much to describe.

But it wasn't life, mucking in slime
anticipating the call to supper.

No dreams goaded us.
Lady bugs kept flying off, and worse,
being swallowed by newts'
very long orange tongues.

August days passed, a toad
on hind legs watching for prey.
My sister's armada was hopelessly stuck in sand.

Why was it always conforting,
pretend forts held so much freedom
but inside our house were rules
that only made us uncontrollable?

My sister kept mustering her battalion
which liked to disperse. That was the problem.
Reality had a will of its own.
She took to reading lines on her palm.

That was it. The world was like war
you couldn't set it straight
before your whole team deserted.
Or: not like war because nobody won.

My sister caught more ladybugs
lying dead ones on a barge.
Adding props, we kept believing what
seemed like what was real.
It never happened. A picture of life was
stubbornly lodged in our brains.

No sharp edge, only a slimy surface.

Inheritance

Earth, febrile and pocked by night.
Why is this sickness unknown?

On our hill, an enormous oak
guardian of cornfields for colonists,
tree of my girlhood adventures
climbing mounting sliding down
now crushed among rocks.

I was a child with a bland face
and a molten mood.
My mother warned, grounding me—
translation: lock me in my room—
her word, preamble to rebellion.

The grand oak, silent, resistant
loomed, billowing a rebel flag.

Prayers to the avenging angel
curses of faithless souls rise
from the miasma of village greens.
Remember I am also an other.

You whose heart is invariant.

We were born to two parents
abuse and absence
one threatens peace,
the other praises heaven

Gladden both with guilt
not responding.

The twin

Come, feel. I stand
beside you, behind you.
No alms needed,
nor hope, nor forgiveness.

Abundance in strife,
breath kept in for stealth
as if action would spy on itself.
To grow free of consequences.

You vanished, near me
by my side, on my bed.
We share refuge in siege
sweet of apple
our mother's lamp, a notebook
glass of water.

Sleep isn't inviting. Listening
for you keeps me sane.

And when day comes—
distrust of dawn
that effaces you from a future
gray in contrition
a beginning that retracts
Will you find another? Will you
abandon me to our cloister
because we are too alike?

Too alike? Sameness
conceals us both.

I am bound to you

voice to tongue.
I am the least difference
truth and imposture.

Will you reject both
for solitude with God

who ghosts your bedside?

CRUISE

Reference

In last analysis, we had only words
to go on. Like magic you could
pull them out of thin air, in darkest moods,
mum even. My ears plugged with ones
like *char* or *bosque* or *pensum.*

Because nobody else was involved,
talking wasn't real talk
but came in folds, gaps, echoes
and traces as happened when
muttered under the breath.
Between us was plain denial.

This was good fortune.
We were leisured and comfortable
though little else was provided
in what life dealt or withheld.
as if we faced the wrong direction
too bent on following
a legacy for which perception
hurried to garner evidence.

Little came. It could happen
only in present time since words
(really, arguments) erased themselves
as though written on water.
Nothing passing left a mark.
Did we love? Was there ambition
or aspiration that moved us?
Did anybody notice our relation?

Questions had their own life.
They lived a phantom time.

We disputed their absence
in bed with righteous intensity.
Nightlight, rug, closet, curtains
all took on ciphered meanings
that left us perplexed.

Trapped, not unhappy,
we wouldn't believe because we knew.
We were blind,
miracle the world really was.
In life it was profaned by
an image of presence.

Conformity, you stink of life.

Terror of absence

There are hours, brief, lurid
that cast a shadow for saints.
They, scattered over a half a life,
two score, glare hypnotically.

The encounters: imprecisely
measured, unlike our thoughts,
pointed words, crumbs
that painfully captured my
meandering attention.

Somehow. The intent
didn't herald a new routine
some formal welcome of kindness
from a neighbor or shopkeeper.

For me the quiet epiphany—
words mumbled in one ear
to come back again and again
axis, I believed, of my inner life.

The hours, pregnant as now.
surreal as a Dali painting, drawn
by a need to suffer fools gladly
that left me numbed to joy
of knowing a response would come,
from the mummy cloth. Eventually.

The non-event would be reason for stuttering.

A world with no stone
across the cave's mouth which forbid
entering or leaving

life as a crucifixion on which nailed
to anxiety,
an anticipation of what must come
because it had to,

came with each phoneme.

Median

A tranquility compromised
grunt of effort challenged.

Debris, a gap torn by
an implosion outerly destructive
visible clouds rise
with smoke from a wildfire.

You, complacency
blending with animal desire,
see rivalry in black and white.

In an instant it died,
the blend of yes and no.
A flash streaked the sky, thought
blazed in the comet's tail: intuition.
Breath involuntary filling.

Afterwards, that trace causes
a shiver, delight that is
calls me forth enduringly, a figure
hillside outlined in relief—
a fur of gold about shoulders
and head, an erstwhile sun.

When is daybreak?

Initiate

A silhouette cut in half.
Doubled light, a lone hand grasps
a porcelain cup bedside,
a metallic jewel box spills.
Beneath the dinner table
one hand finds an other.

I kneel by a bench as if to pray.
A wind harp amplifies
silent remembering remorse.

At what cost of feeling,
to forgive the weakness
to be alone—impossible—that
shames all efforts at beauty?
Disgrace.

Assigned house cleaning
while he pretends schoolwork
starring as 'the good one',
does he feel his the more malicious?

How would he feel vacancy
if I were to leave?
His body pulses
as an other passes by
more lightly than a cloud
touches the air.

Sensation escapes
doubled, augmented in voice
perfecting lyrics to a song
that died twenty years ago.

Life itself, starved for contact
hunger, pain—
work to which he is devoted.
Mistrust of ambition.

What I found too late:
backseat of our family car.
Rain drumming the roof on pause
as thunder drowns an inaudible promise
to feel love pass through.

Did it signify joy for both?
His meekness, his daydreams,
he has not been moved
by her tears, their suppressed fury.

He was alive.
He has felt his singleness,
divided by duplicity

of one who cunningly asks 'Who?'

Dandelion wine

If I could, if I warned you
before when we were free,
though earth bound us,
you would honor my thought,
logical and persuasive.

Nobody told me. My aunt was
boiling a thick stew of dandelion
gathered from the back yard
where her sheep grazed.

Steam rose with a frantic cry,
droplets clung to cracked paint
to rain on the overworked stove.

She added sugar by tablespoons
at a time, her sister, my mother,
sipped a glass of chartreuse liquid

us tasting, counseling one another;
aromatic spring clouded judgment
color chastened to midnight green,
its own litmus test.

We sat lost in giggles, especially you
who had a taste for wine.

Into the dank atmosphere, I disappeared
lured by senses inward,

alive, illegible. As my aunt
weighed a final judgment,

I became gravity of honey
when its substance fills the calyx
of a lily and over.

My life suspended in face of
mystery, its rankled scent.

Wineglasses catch late winter sun
filtered through windows sweating.

No one had warned me of how,
sugaring fruit becomes spirit.

They might have said:
you'd want to die for more,

Bless weightless matter, drink,
sleeper, push your tongue
deeply into the bottle. Live.

Earth needs your feeling. Impassable
simple presence, never flinching.

It will keep you alive,
wet gloss on your lips.

Simulacra

The law is, like likes like
though it is years to bear fruit
since difference exists: one
a professor, the other a political hack.
More: one has money, one not.
One disheveled, the other glamorous.
Both read Homer, one in Greek.
The spouses adore each other
and exchange secrets of their bed.

When they turn to facts
(at a New Years party), it is a turn
to fate, a predestined birthing
in the classical sense both knew
(from different teachers) and argued
the meaning that ancients gave.
to this new life—teachers of capacious minds
informed by deep love
of humanity, miscreants and saints alike—
they learned to think generously.

It ended with relating what
years had wrought, how experiences
molded them, often the same in
nuanced ways, as if life came
with factory settings for different models
(both suffered fear of failure)
and how important divergence was
since in speaking of past regrets,
fear of copying another's sins
was a means of owning an identity
certain and never avowed.

As destiny excites interest
on another level, novel feelings of
respect and tolerance arose.
Neither had experienced it.
Pain had bruised each
to a tenderness that could take in
the other's preference with no bitterness.

Sisterhood, a late arrival.

Ambitions

Each while left a stain.
Who designs that? Dozing
in bed languid, driven no longer
by 'the burn', not unfulfilled

we planned to stay as we were
in place, not ahead or
back. Desireless, a hinge swinging
in calm of a cyclone,
sage in emotional surges.

It effaced maturity.
Our children suffered and their friends.
They grew wild, lacked ambition
or had strange urges that did damage.

We fixed our house, painted
bedrooms, did landscaping. We
entertained, visited Europe, not friends.
There were pets and chores
put off week to week.

Of ourselves, little was asked.
What could have conflicted was
glossed over. Things faded in wind
were fit with indelible plans.
To say we adapted was wrong.
We followed no one's counsel since
we knew it errant. Nor did we
criticize: our tongues cut out.

Innocents perish
behind a façade of equanimity.

Regarding judgment, we reeked of it.

Between crossword puzzles, we worried
about being good Germans. An
expression we used. What mercy
we did, around campfires, while listening
to news, reading each other's books
doing civic affairs, we disavowed.
We couldn't bear what we were.

Oddly, history proved right.
There were things we wanted—
guilt, for instance. Our children
protested the addiction
with disdain they felt for our values

especially that we asked little
in their pursuits.
The flower in the crannied wall
roused sufficient pleasure.
that we cared to not display it. . .

Yet our children diminished
fully sunk into their posts
like rocks around our campfire pit
as though our impassable being
gave them little to search for,
as if old age, its facticity,
lacked rapture altogether.

Sirens' song

Half-drunk wine bottle,
street sounds climb skyward like vapor.

In reverie, lying on a sheet
tangled, an empty bed, alone
tensed for footfalls.

I was in love, fatuously
an owl on silent wings
pursuing it, wanting *nada*
not your touch, not your smell.

It sufficed, wine, shuffle
of clothes, thrum of commerce.
For hours warm spring air
leeched through a cracked window.

The breeze picked a low note
drying the bottle's rim.
It gave an *om*, fulfillment.
My thoughts were rarefied
as they bleached luxuriously out.

I watched clouds scud by
tops of office buildings. My blood pulsed
with their supple speed.

You were unworried I remained.
Exalted moods mattered little to us.

I woke at noon, with lies
prepared for work and stories

for a sense of normality
People looked like angels.

It sufficed. Before evening, a grey
rain began. The storm rewrote
drama, a few hours with a stranger.
Sighs, texture on flesh, *nirvana*.

Afterwards I bought Chinese food
to bring home to you,
enduring the moan of the half-empty bottle—

calling one's eternity to it?

The nucleus

We were a family,
pointed to in lectures as such,
mythic, from the old world
in an emotional clamp of relations
each noble but brittle. I thought
otherwise. Bloodline was reprisal
a band of ghosts.

My brother and I, walk-ons.

The Berkshires. Nor'easters
blew down trees, breached
the chimney with rain, buckled floors.
I watched tall hickories
sway like pickup sticks, stiff but flexible.
The house, I hoped, similarly.

One has to consider with care.
My mother didn't drive.
Normally we played at home.
There wasn't choice: it was
who we were, we were told. Most life
was that dead end: turns at
washing dishes, school with black
and white saddle shoes.

Our mother had distinct views
culled from *Readers' Digest*
of what a child was in need of
irrespective of its own impulse.

Rules of appearance: clean dress.
Rules of attitude: strive upward.

Rules of self: privacy,
doubt, pretense for others
who see a calm, affective you.

Storms seemed to barrel through.
Same with adolescence, labyrinths
threaded, better the dark pit
than the black alley.
Walls were meant to contain us.

Ballet lessons. My brother
on the violin. Bikes, farm animals
heavy downpours loosening roots
dewfalls to wash away phantasms.
Any change in form
added danger to our sterile rounds
through cobwebbed hallways.
Dust, holy glow of a candle.
Love was when we strayed from safe.

Tremor in summer storms.
We grew into that fury.
Rivalry was its term.
Life had only a single winner.

My brother let me hold him
when wind rocked furniture
its moldering upholstery.
He had a glass eye.

We were children.
Neither of us knew
the blood inheritance.
He trembled, he cried for love.

I tried to return it.

Appeal

The dark glass. As we look,
so we're seen..

What made us
paused between two breaths,
a windripple that dropped us,
locked the door: with family.

A trace memory, less than water's.

Vortex of household, cold air
the mother crying from pain, body
misshapen, monstrous in bed.

Blades of grass between two fingers,
pucker for whistling,
a fire pit, skewers of roasted lamb.

At climax, shrieks drowned
amniotic fluids,
muscular push unveils a world.

Do I anguish? Suspecting
hell is built by human hands.
An intent unmakes us. Dark wind
in my brain. You, deaf-mute dreamer,
who must return, to pay
my ransom. How can I myself?

Exodus

Leaves narrow the wet road.
Light seeks a maze to thread
streetlight first, then sun.
Pattern shifts not because
of earth's vagaries
but the atmosphere's inconstancy.

Red zinnia in cloisonné.
Water drop by drop from the eaves.
Geese hasten to parse blank sky.
Hours after, howl of a dog

raga of monstrous shiverings,
disquiet itself. Milkweed
blown in, out, in, behind curtains.
The mind a muscle, tensing,
dilating, taking it to heart.

When a single word, meek obedience,
stammered through my mouth
agrees with no real intent to obey,
iridescent wings blanch the air.

Midday. In its breeze,
a memory perfuse as ragweed—
with rippling ribbon tail of a kite.
Forms are announced to follow.

The road dry, swept clean.
Geese invent the letter 'v'.

Then, road wet imprints of
leaves, an intaglio. . .

exodus a people.

Protection

Sarcasm learned young
taught us to deflect,
never feel a right to speak
to others who knew,
never see anything but
blunt avidity in a child.

One exception lay in the matter
of gratitude,

You added *thank you* to each
morsel received, to acknowledge
how poor you really were,

never allude to badlands
or deserts in your moods:
words would be held against us.

What does one forgot?
That one felt *owed* a ration of joy
which was freely given?

Judgment joined deprivation
taught grace of disgrace.

Contrition disabled us
like penciled understrokes
that ruin a canvas,
the obvious made obvious,
which is to say we wept.

Disdaining the angels.
repeated (under breath) our tractates

on human evil. On each other's
breast we saw the scarlet badge.

From city fumes and decibels,
tranquil, drowsily
peace comes on doves' feet,
opening eyes to dawn light,
we surrender
least happiness.
in flesh of a fruit.

Our acquiescence.

Toward hibernation

Cobwebs waft on the vent grill,
spiders belay above asphalt roofs
frost wilts tomato plants but come dawn,
like a heavy dream, melts—
charity of whitening.

Deeper, older tensions
cleave to bone, unfaltering.
Sweep crackling seedpods
mauve blossoms into thick air:
normal in a grown-up way.

Reality ceases being virtual,
renewed weighted for flight,
ribbon tail of a lizard.
Christmas cactus blooms.

Has the bid been met?
In words, counting-rhymes let go
dance-games in the magic box?

A nuthatch searches oak bark
pocked spores of lichen.

The season taken back
Silks, furs, feathers, our enormous wings
lift to us this dark season
clutch of incarnation
gifted without invoice.

Day cactus blooms red suns.
A slender vase of being
consents to touch.

Guardian

I never believed I was chosen.
It was my other self.

I was foolish. I asked for fame.
Fame came with an asterisk
in a record book.

I asked for comfort, absence of pain.
Illness resulted. Disbelief
confirmed my guardian

played with my words, garbling
insinuating meanings,
in short, lying on my behalf,
for a purpose that escaped me.

My words must have sounded banal,
intent missing, residue of
a passion to summarize the other
imagining wants
but mostly fears, desertion.

Due to these failures, I often
spoke with the angel
ecstatic with her choice of pronouns
laboring, I supposed, to appeal to
my idiom and become
more fluent with my true self.

As a child thwarted, I did not hear
due to damaged eardrums.
Most others, I saw, suffered the like

As though we too were guardians—
blind leading blind—of a virtue
at home with well-being.

It was a revelation. We were nurses
and orderlies of love,
able to diagnose wishes of the ill
because of life-long training.

A future came clear.
Preparing, repairing: my guardian
offered a course to master grief.

My words grew studied (to compress
my story) blunt, straight-forward
so that an infant would get it.

If I was bound to a hysteric
life-preserver for my tears,
I was at least impassioned martyr
to a drama played to no other audience.

In the workaday world, I barely spoke.
Words were to be divined. Ascendant
were days, crystal nights'
silent fusion. They lacked all witness.

I became becoming

The visit

Age showed my secret wish.
I dream no more.

Strange, old age was magnetic
drawing to it life before its time.

Time amplified through memory.
I went back.
The house, smaller, not clapboard.
Board and batten, door frame splintering.

Trees were taller, hickory, oak,
not shrubby alder and birch.
Boyhood friends had married,
moved to city jobs. Or were dead.
Much needed mending.
I wasn't a repairman.

The yard was what I knew,
rutted to car tires.
Stores were filled with townies
who greeted me as intruder.

It was a postcard memory,
stone driveway, house bundled into
the lane, exact down to details

to be set moving by some act—
involuntary or chance—
attesting to a pump room
where a hiding place vanished,
closet for a solitary's prayer
his caged heart feeling.

A boy passes through me
hurrying to be grown,
the man's body-mind
hovers over fathomless waters.

This is how life came,
where I find it still
invisible screen just behind
the past remembered.

Voices

We listened to one another
only when imperative.
That way, negligence, tempting us,
was no offense. Voices
time-travel across warps in space.

Indecision was
a mottled voice that roused feelings
in the silvery now of life,
in coexistence with abandon,
terror at missed contact.

How separated, when real,
(one lives in another city) or
ideal (virtual nature of an other)
leaves you unable

to be at ease in social scenes
and so, doubts regarding intent
probably erotic in nature—
roused concern for hidden motives.

Certainly there was a distorted
(if slightly) version of reality. We
no longer shared place, time—
familiarity vanished, muffled
by words of a foreign language.

It was a first. Intimacy with
no one. Yet to implore
to be received deeply within.
An epiphany so subtle it went unnoticed
except for questions it quelled.

Impermanence. So that after,
memory made had stories
about what might have happened.

One of a kind. But the whole thing
would begin all over once more
at a certain interrogation:
'Are you there?' 'Will you speak?'

until it became self-evident
that a haphazard universe
permits no constancy
because the grating voice of need
bellows, speaking in tongues
of the luck not to need luck.

A body, scrambling
a voice that would guide us
to the one thing needful.

Habit

Those who knew us well saw
how distinction lured each,
a tilt of the neck as if
in an imagined conversation
freighted with profundity
the body's movements
heavy, disjointed, lending
an air of absent intelligence.

Life surge forward
lingeringly drawn to quiet city streets
a cottage with few windows, leisure of
long nature walks. It liked
a home tidy, flowers
at bedside, coffee black,
music neither classical nor pop.
Best of all night at three a.m.—
innocent murmuring
the other's words—
what is your name/ You know
I'm not allowed to say.

At proper intervals, witch hazel bloomed,
cichorium risen from dead leaves.
Cold rain put fields up fallow,
hungry for preservation.

Impulsively life wished to return,
whether or not triumphant,
wayfaring unavoidable disasters
invited when attention lapsed,
which was often.

Yes, the island. Bay stretched
to horizon. Blue beyond,
waves distilled light purer than the sun's,
whales breach magnificently—
angels drop their disguises
to prove dreams cogent.

The mind's dream. The same two,
sun and waves, the same street
the same apples on display
book, silver spoon (a legend),
now known, perceived with humility,
no longer cloud a pathway
that blessings happily line.

What sacred word does my life
utter to bring itself forth?

Glass between two moon

I was born retrograde,
between two moons, a star-child
I grew up with virtue
along with my unnamed twin.
News barely touched us.

I read obsessively, with a view
toward personal destiny
tolerated by my family who
lectured me against fixed ideals.

There was no rule against writing
though words withered
on my indifferent right hand,
I lived in fear of a poor opinion
in my twin's mind—
her brow furrowed, brows arched against me.

In any event, a viewpoint
set me apart from her
since she was known as critical.

Our language used few words:
clash, gather, subdue, resent.

They ordained a life.

Starlight

Frost salted lawns, a white scrim
melting contours hillside.
A wound once concealed wouldn't heal.
Color added the sun, then warmth,
then after baited breath, vanished
into mist to leave stubble upright, dead.
Out from within, people walked,
arm in arm, at times listening
to the other. Much was burdened
about this way of being
baker, builder, milliner, slave.

That dawn we came out.
You do not accept our origin.
We are the same item. Brusque.
Questioning. Seek what can't be found,
loved for being elusive.

Soon shadows browse alleyways,
in evening, men and women find
dalliances that linger toward bed.
A moon rises, harvest with a second frost.
In roots of grasses, earthworms
pursue their needful existence.
Raging, foxes's screams find
prey in dreams of children.

What of our holy aspirations
that persist, lacking proof?
What risk, becoming mad?

Frost muzzled predation,
frozen in a leap.

Facts remained hard and fast.

You spoke inaudible words.
I could hear clearly as
mice shrieking at the fox's dinner.

Last prayer.

A vision

From a future, I warn
with a word I can't now say
(*love*)
because it mustn't be read..

You in whose bed I sleep,
whose soul is my body,
whose lips have found ways
to quell my heart's disquiet.

I was anxious. Wind rasps
at a window. Uncles
and aunts in my grandfather's
living room peer through a glass magnifier
at the Dumont TV. War images
from a country of rice paddies.
Forkfuls, my grandmother's potato kugel,
cousins exchange judgments, glasses
clink, aroma of stewed apricots,
marzipan in shapes and colors of fruits.

Intensity lifts a bottle
of amber liquid from a cupboard,
my grandfather poised to refill,
kitchen light fluorescent—
window suddenly empties the sky,
gray, its existence suspended.

Deep contentment. Love of life,
intense embrace
of sense, terror emerges from joy.
Tears streak my cheeks,

my grandfather pauses his rounds,
my mother's consoling words.

I wasn't sad. I wanted nothing
but to be alone with sensation
into which I vanished
no remainder. Only feeling
so familiar I seemed one with me
No thoughts. I was safe
identity protected no longer.

Outside, a branch still scrapes.
My grandfather pours.
Laughter blanks out the TV image.

About miracles, how
a thing ends or another begins,
cunning of quicksilver. I didn't realize
feeling gets lost, a gift
in softly wrapped longings.
This I want to say to you.

You will be sad. You will be happy.
You will seek what can't be yours.

As you grow old, you will want
to be wounded deeper,
to sweep up anguish
with a wing-tip.

The earth is patient. It has time to kill.

It will enslave you, addict,
with beautiful trinkets.

BERTHING

Night walk

Beacons at night, glow worms,
lycopodium, black bark of birch,
puff balls, galactic nebulae.
Walking cloaked, gliding
over dry leaves, silence pulverized.
Earth, a rock face, watches
your asylum with indifference.

Is this the place?

Circles of holy stone are near as
marrow of our love,
near as Draco
who watches hunger
a circle of coyotes tightens.

We waited for shooting stars.
No further conversation.
Sky reflected in waterglass
shows a cliff, specked with galaxies.
The face glowered radioactively,
sparks thrown to the abyss.

We waited with thirst, poor at ease.
In the end, it felt disappointing
no show of heaven.

Your hands would never murder
or forgive or sustain. A thin moon, a
twin, and earth trade photons. Stars
hold inquisitions. In ourselves
unsaid is a farewell they restate:
in fire, incandescence.

Restraint in longing. Sensation
suffering consciously,
to not leave what we most care for.

Our remorse was spent, stained
with confessions.

At first sincere, the
second covered over.

Myopia

I was going blind. Before long
my sockets would be white eggshells.
At school, I begged
not to read, not to recite
runes once was written.
Homer left relics of the same disease.

I was wounded before birth.
Childhood swaddled in
a closed definition.
But of what, I did not know.
Family members likely intuited
I adored pity.

It was hidden suffering,
streaming phantomic prayers.
The eye doctor prescribed glasses.

Social concerns were worse
than physical pain. I bore taunts.
I could see a golden thread,
that if followed would turn my grief
to memorable words.
Like Milton.

In bed, my throat clogged
when I couldn't make tears.
Destiny stole my adolescence
a caul child in its place.
In bind of language
was I a poet frightened by words?
Conscience was no condolence.

Pity left, sorrow gained voice
amused at my misfit.

Was I aware, days and months
through seventy years, even now,
who I was when spoken to?
The dead living under my front porch,
you think I don't know your name,
your dog tag?

A portent wracked my body.
An obsession written in blood.

I gave myself to you.
You made concessions. I haven't.
I read your notes,
slave to a conceited sibilance.

It is only chemistry.

Custody

Several indictments
with aging, denied then reprieved
are arrested in your word.

Then I was perceptive
who collected things
likely to be persuaded
there was no secret evidence.
I burrowed beneath surfaces.
I split rocks until they set me free.

These hours consume the same
crusts of bread, bowls of sour wine
cheese crusts of horned goats.

I bore the brunt of interrogations
while others went untouched

in ecstasy of learning
from a fount that provides comfort.

Bread baked unleavened, last
meal engorged with no blessing.

Does it then sustain me?

In one book, earth was
new and stainless,
but there was no sea to cross, only
rankled cities to leave.

I was a slave.
I begged to join the exodus

ecstasy between two moons.

With others I followed, guided, led.
Watched.

I was deceived.

Pure memory

Cellar stairs, an endless
drop onto Army boots on top of
Eisenhower jackets.
A rat's nest, really.
Ballistics had been altered:
steps metal not wood. Flowers
perennial, peonies, foxglove.
But the neighborhood—families of
boyhood—was new. Fence
and gate reinstated property lines.
Owners were half my age.

A smell, the Sound's
faintly fetid air, remembers.
It drowns in fresh macadam.

Differences have come to be less different.
Memory is true: house,
driveway that hewed to the lane,
sleepy Yankee cow town.

An direct image, no twists
but enjoyed, consumed
in avowal of
time's cut and nearness
to the immemorial.

Barefoot? I walk free.

Schooling

Cells' *faux* eternity,
split endlessly in halves.

I am a cell.

My belongings:
a chessboard, pawns
alert to adversity.
An antique tobacco tin
for coins that bulges full
one rare buffalo nickel.
Two pairs of skates,
one laced to the other.

On a squat altar,
candle wax, hinting myrrh.
Waning rippled moonlight.

Us two, never at once, kneel
before an unknown Madonna
mother of coy blessings
for the meek twin aloof
with her hoped for grace.

After the classroom he tries
to parse grammar
his teacher puts on the board,
others giggle behind his back.
Try edges of his shame.

How he learns:.
read, idealize, apply.

Because driven by ideals
feelings sink to anger.

No one flies to assist victory.

What makes a rivalry?
One is the missing other,
dreamed double,
Shiva with extra limbs
dances inside encircling flames:
he keeps their petition.

Ashes turn to common dust,
gleaming seduction.

When cold comes, it is difficult.
Covers piled, wind through walls,
he remembers other tremors,
lover's, hosanna, *post coitum*
emptiness, vertigo
divided unevenly in two—
now danced, sustained, *felt*.

Sobriety of witness.

He has attested, erotically,
frankincense confirms
the herb's exalting presence
wakes the oracle in him,
rebel warrior poet.

The affair

Then it leaped to day one, spring.

Room in a landmark hotel
taxi from airport.

We drank in the backseat
from a wine bottle.

The whole night? Rapture, plastic
cups on a bronze tray. Emptied,
a breeze turned them melodic.

Love-making dared an open balcony.
Downtown gladdened with traffic,
'in joy' for us. It was as though
a band mounted some Dylan song,
soft lyric on air.

If one could die of bliss. Mouths
impatient for arrival. Hunger
left me poorer, graced by desire
bestowed rejoicingly at midnight.

Then, unsated passion turned
terror improbably triggered
by saying *love*. We dozed
lifted over a dawn nimbus
two of us in one skin.

A minor achievement. The impression
decades after poignancy
had no face. A sole image:

an empty bottle of malbec,
a windowsill, dewfall.

Office day in dirty clothes.

Crises

Time like space, no third dimension.
Fever-ridden body in damp bedclothes,
I inhabited it, walls collapsed.

Under a gong on the headboard,
I slept, cord in hand.
My mother elsewhere, one ear cocked.

Outside it snowed. A chill crept
through blankets, into my mangled body.
Feeling flaccid, an atmosphere
pressed down, touching, suffocating.
I was an inert corpuscle.

Windows had veils.
I lay on one elbow reading.
The gong I chose
to ignore. I would be a pilgrim
ignorant of acts to sanctify
my pain and make it holy.

Ice storm. Weeks went by
schooldays forgiven, foregone.
I wept, daydreams
incubus of a soul, kept
walls closing in.

The fever broke. My mother laughed,
gong removed. Abruptly, spring,
windows flung open, a cat on the pillow
curious about smells.

I was robust. Then I was a man

with a wife, a job, a family.
Time wasn't reluctant, it pushed
for a finish, whatever that was.
It held a goad for driving beasts
to pasture. There was no escape.

All the same I was a boy, delirious.
Death threatened. I lived an oblivion
where trust was kept in a safe.
I strayed around halls of heroes
and saints, yellow wallpaper,
wax and wane of the moon,
terror and belonging,
hoped for, shunned.

After, days were sunny.
my clock, to its measure,
foreshortened to a vanishing point.

The injury left a scar,
the scar a denial to be.

Purging

Pulsing at my temples.
Will it become migraine?
Heated air from the register
slakes it, my lover's breathing—
name lost—asks riddles in my ear.
Words unable to be felt.

Letters with wayward passion
under rules for 'politic expression.'
A waste basket chokes early versions.
At a gas station, a motel behind.
A number of men, some strangers, bus stations
movie lobbies, the village hall.
Right postage was essential.
Dignity must remain intact on breakage,
incomplete bestowal.
I was good at ghosting.

It was art nonetheless. It repeated life,
rounding corners, dulling edges
marking endings (that don't exist).
It taught, not by repetition ('mirror')
but surrender, one face hostage to another.
Meaning does express a countenance.

Great monuments bereft of
the stone of solitude before heart
is turned flesh—under anesthesia—
haggard, rouged, lit by fire,
though I sought through their marks
on my breast my lovers'
as fluty notes from the furnace
did acapella with the air.

Earth was frozen, stillness
of daily rounds, astonishment
at flux of vitality
that alters the river's course,
a minute gap to mind
in which death cells gather.

Do not enter.

Hurricane

A windrose. A whinny, then a rumble,
stating reservations. The sun's
mirage of a farther shore.
People given to imagine
a comet's flight along
an indefinite zenith had
eyes and ears for ordinary things
making dinner, sweeping floors.

The same storm brought beings like us.
A cipher, a broken algorithm
Even though you deny it. We are rebels,
Your impulse to make war real.

Sunlight, its unflinching ascent.
People pose for work, wind
dies to a loose rattle. The lawn
is dense with migrating birds.
A mass of tangled staccatos.

What of our search for faith,
fault-line beneath pretension
a breach between?
The homily of being human.

Clatter dies, leaves no legacy.
Without which our bruises ache,
in lack of cause for being.

We, the dispossessed.

Sickness

You entered through the rear door.

I in the window seat
count cars below.

A trance, a delirium
brought me to the doctor's.
I was feverish, without pain.

To prod wasn't part of the exam.
I wanted proof:
chair creaking, radiator hissing
my ears as well,
minute after minute, counter-questions.

I needed little more.
'Else' was a framing word.

Snow fell in bands around streetlamps.

You were preoccupied. You let me
live because you were obligated to.

By the end, your mood lightened. I did
what you do afterwards. I put clothes back on
with dignity though my heart
was in my mouth, mucous membranes
coated thoughts.

The doctor's advice, a pat
on my shoulder, a script of paper.
I stuffed it in a back pocket.

Afterward, it crumbled in a fist.
I wondered whose found poem it would be.

What was needed: to feel
song that excels that of birds.

Confession

I loved a man once.
I loved a woman once,
I loved both twice
in both my body found itself
the perfect double
as an amoeba in mitosis.
My desire followed suite.

I tired. Multiple was conventional,
not freakish but a praxis.
In that, I discovered the neutral
which you and I perfected
deflowered intimacy.

Communion across oceans
back and forth flashing code.
You shared Henry James, I was reading
Virginia Wolfe, we met at some middle.

Of course it was banal
not a famous correspondence
stuck in history books.
My letters plotted seduction—
showing wounds in need of care
that expressed self-cruelty—
contradictions dangled a hook.

Later I saw they were too true
to turn into poems.

A dose of derision. A dose
of irony. Declaring truth per se
came with a grain of salt

or a slant.

I loved a man once. I loved
him twice, the two names he gave.
Then I tired of listening
that lacked know-how.

The whirlwind had dizzied me,
leavening by vicarious love
aerated in far-away train stations—
words I would attach
to a gravel voice in my head,
brother born with me
but for the actuary's calculus.

Pain realized in
banality of my delight
its plan hidden in a purse,
I like a pickpocket
who sees only pockets on the saint.

I never congratulated you
for the hand-written verse
that was published. My drawings
at the local library sale
would have impressed you.

You were faithful
though I suspected
enthusiasm was your own evasion.

I loved a man, a woman. I loved both.
Though love never bore fruit,
I was loyal. The letter
kept as an exemplary case.

In some sober mood,
I will reread the story
oceanside, great waves cresting.

It will let me feel a vagrant,
Intense, monumental.

I once loved a man or a woman.
I became one of each.
I became.

Survival

Under the old threat, only two of us
came in with powers.
Some stronger, some weaker,
it depended on who was going down.
And, we went, you and I,
with different wills.

Powers drew on competing means.
That meant obstacles and frustrations
were unknown beforehand.

In struggle, the weaker
was without aspiration,
collateral damage of descent.

Forebodings, loss, ardent hope
drowned in thirst for experience,
the child's eyes denied
an impression that revealed her type:
non-empathetic.

Out of sync with intention
though you retain each memento
joyous or morbid, that you have of us.

Repetition repeated
us infallibly put on diverging courses
though none else was probable.
True, our survival reflex over-reacted,
when we wanted happiness.
We were saboteurs.

As a concession, we felt it

blink away (withholding a sign)—
posture of conformity.

We took a victory lap,
a new power that wasn't ours,

the unknown.

Phantoms

Impulses ghost; we furnish haunts.

Let loose, they slip into our brains
dinning thought. In chambers
of the heart.

They affected some grand schemer. She
plotted a world 'and all therein'
including you and me.

A contrivance got us here,
no alternative acceptable.

Delights *in utero*, dropping in fecal soup.
Milk, sweet and heavy. Medicinals.

We live now on earth. Make earth live.
Mud and microbes, tidal pools.

Before whirlwinds of dust
spoke scriptural words,
cells carried air gingerly through culverts.
crannies and sinkholes.

We waited inside this mute cavern,
purpose shrouded.
Desires of the father on the mother.
Desires for our obedience.

I have ambitions never sought.

Why this way? Why
doesn't love suffice?

Desires rage in phantom veins
in likeness of a heart.

You now bear exile
from the body,

slave.

The order of things

Azure veils high autumn,
morning a tedious maze,
late chamerion, asters.
Leaves make the road narrower.

Imperative. Made to,
protest justice, tune out.

At night it froze. Rims
of ice enchain the puddles.
I felt terror: loss of identity.

It passes sweetly. Roads widen.
Hoarfrost ceases to blanch nut grass.

Geese arrive in braces.
Ground forgives frost, softened; earthworms
work prodigiously. We no longer hold
our breath for warmth.

In summer, earth repented.
Pathways, trees to hide in.
We had safety in pleasure.

Weather that our lives
pursue, a squirrel chased
around a tree until it is
the trunk that turns
world in tow, us on it,
but tenderly, grip never wavers.

Nerves at autumn's
breakdown in harvest.

Then I woke. Suffering
hunger, it became imperative
to break the sacred lock of my cell.

To whisper *open sesame.*

Joy

The blessed need little beyond
their blessing. When my life was a-shambles
I still knew goodness
in my suffering.

I learned to ask.
Not for desire's elixir
but everyday spirits that console.
What I got had expired, worthless.

I learned to risk joy. Then I could
beg my guardian, listing specifics.
Were there any? Her response depended.

Tenses challenged me, spelling
hazardous, intent cloaked.
At times, negation didn't appear at all
except in its double.
Which made me ask whether language
issues came with a laxity
not found in ancient days.

Warped in time, my wishes were
premature and spoke indirectly
demanding response in kind.

This inference brought great calm
since I no longer felt singled out
or owed (more or less) a beneficence

But higher principles
obligated, namely
lessons for impatient souls like myself,

and for my part, a too human
acquiescence to divine purpose that
overlooked unvoiced reservations.

It was a breakthrough. We (the angel
and myself) were collaborators
in righting the world,

piecing together needs
compatible with heavenly designs.
How simple it all was!

A response from our communion
would be an entry in a thesaurus,
culling words for future linguists.

Truth could be gleaned from error,
fault from sincerity, others would
be helped by a new standard in purity.

I asked for more. I asked for less.
I revised and counter-signed.
My appeals grew self-referential

each sentence built on the last
in shape of a syllogism,
unarguable, certain, beautiful

like a pharaoh with a golden tongue.

I had redacted time.

The other time

By fall, days brought to dust
wrappings dulled by persistence.
Their drift was a story
in a story, words being entire chapters.
In dustfall, our lives double back.

Each mood had its reverse side
measured in separateness
that found it bitter, though
a communion, still virtual,
our diversions, in bad taste.

After a week, common experience,
at low intensity,
sun strayed behind dust clouds
shone in shadings and hue.

It was a phenomenon, a sign,
a riddle: the apex of a love
prefigured in years of reverie.

Time distended not unlike the present.
Bloating was joyous when our paths
crossed the forbidden, full of feeling
since being alive lit our minds,
self-made generosity by forgoing
its band of private urges.

The journal entry of a day ran pages.

A clarity that resisted change endured
so that, called back, our days remembered
absolute freshness

as though, in an eddy, flux ceased.
I could face tides of change
given wholly to perceived events.

The old normal made new.

Celestine

At ten, I was distinguished.
I believed in signs
by which I meant, from the stars.
A glowering ball of dust one time lingered
overhead, traversing my dead father's lawn.

I read my calling, not distinctly
it was unsigned.
Like Galileo, I would find new worlds
in longitude closer to angels.

I cried tears for want of a spy glass,
feeling cheated of a vocation
boyhood full of grief—
destruction was golden.

My family remained ignorant
while anguish gnawed at my adolescence.

Yet some part was relieved
since Galileo died by fire,
I would have been set aflame
but for my parents' disaffection.

Refrain of boyhood:
orbits of planets, constellations
of heavenly bodies. I was a spy,
the cosmos spoke, I would burn
rather than recant my findings.
In bed before sleep, I retraced occultations
but glory of discovery was dim.

It is otherwise, sixty years after

dark dreamy watches,
the screen, intricacies of human veins
flashpoints of feeling-
light linger in sidereal extinction, then
the black wool shroud of eulogy.

At ten, I knew life contained fame
and death, but I had it wrong.
Fascination with stars rose from cells
of my body, their unlit nuclei
under hawthorn and willow
divining truth instead.

Slant

Practiced, my mind repeats
the news. As I slept
one ear on my lover's chest
as unfathomable scenes played
in my remembering.

A drawerful of journal entries
needs one staple to be a book.
There were volumes spoken.
Plots with hurried stage whispers,
hotel rooms with leaky faucets
men with unpronounceable family names.
tickets to Europe, reserved, unpaid.
Self-image preserved. Truth in its slant
correspondently the life
never tried on or fitted.

When pages were read,
writing was mimed and flat.

Isn't the mirror the point? To hold
the required angle to what life brings?
Not workings of chance but
form, barely visible, that purpose takes
so as to trace guidelines
left drafting the vision.

Love, solitude, sun on white birch bark,
grand imponderables dissected
in schools where my forbearers taught.
From them, my thoughts haven't strayed.

Convalesces of the everyday.

Sisters of my night, sorrow and joy,
can I feel you grind
and grind salt from the magic box
pouring into the endless sea?

No magic word to stop it.

Lunacy

Quintessence: at midnight.
Flinging nets of clouds,
stars drop their chicanery
becoming stories undreamt
protagonists in a riddle war.
Failure to answer, fatal.

The moon came up crooked
overly round, wrinkled,
whiting out details
of human life I'd waked to see:
a simple landscape, much ado.
The rest—war, dread, hunger—
lay behind locked doors.
Terrible particulars were graced
to the stars in whose deep sphere
prayers were salvaged.

I stood neck craned,
expecting strength and support.
Constellations would glide
week by week, cold, eternal flickerings
rhythmically coded
portents that bore witness
to the curvature of earth,
to claim dominion
over human thought.

I searched the horizon
for a fainter point of brightness,
a presence that felt needful.
I stared in indifference
that feigned tranquility and accepted it.

Calm of infinity, army of suns
to be counted before sleep.
They were repentant. I was not.
Under them I rejected my faults
which were not numerous, and took in
qualities I lacked; courage, endurance.

All that weighed me down
was absorbed in celestial dust
and returned to mitosis.

One half inevitably stillborn.

Proposal

Winter came
a single icicle dangled
its flashpoint of many suns

a crystal windowpane, breath blue.

We made love then.
We made love over again, many days.

Smell of new-fallen snow.
Groans of lake ice.
Taste of frozen maple sap
on the lips.

With summer, I was distraught.
Earth warmed burrows of the fox.

Garden iris bloomed,
magenta and yellow. I picked several stalks
to release myself from feeling.

There was love, improbably.
There were cherries in autumn.
We would walk in evening's filigree.

I held your hand.
You held my hand.

Winter came and again.
Dawn was compromised.
Our hands parted as I watched
brown spots darken.

The birth had its Salome.

Outer space

After camp, my brother got school books
Neighborhood games happened by chance.
No TV past bedtime. He was old
enough for the bus, meaning abuse
from bigger boys who learned it at home.

Home was an argument you couldn't win.
Days began seeking how.
You learned accounting
with a ledger like an actuary,

figures my mother confirmed
while she cooked dramatic meals, house-cleaned
and made babies like us two.

My brother liked stars. He sneaked
after bedtime to make 'observations.'
He wanted it to be winter
when constellations were brightest.

Hours dragged. Eyes closed, I stayed
in bed, digesting his abandon.

I could see his tan hat in houselight,
his thin silhouette in moonlight.

When he returned toward dawn,
I memorized his face framed
by his baby blanket.

I would have come along
but he never asked. Sleep didn't appeal
even after the alphabet game.

Neither did night, which came earlier.
I didn't want new saddle shoes
or a lunch box.

They were blood money paid
for complacence at school.

The truth was, I saw through it.
We were poured into a mold, emerging
in a spotless kitchen
with more babies.

I wanted my brother to know.
While he was doing baseball
I read about Sarah Bernhardt
with a flashlight under the blanket.

Cold left frost on the lawn.
My brother had to wear boots
for his observations, returned shivering.
Stars were bright and active as were
coyotes howling at them.

Then silence froze night.
Winter was passing.
We were growing up.

My mother forgot to tell me.
I learned it wasn't up to me.
Someone else was in charge.

Years sped up. Tempo carried
us, racing now, then slowing
under stage lights, prompted by a chorister,
applause, a back door exit,
at last onto the eternal fire escape.

My mother at the kitchen counter
set out our usual breakfast.

We ate cereal from boxes.

Blindness

Heaven above, dearth below.
Between: one world.
Does nature abhor an empty heart?

On Belden Hill a shagbark tree.
Site of my boyhood blindness.
An asset I couldn't then see.

I was marked with an eye wound
that caused tearful aggression.
My father used Army techniques
but restraint didn't work. Apparently
it poured gasoline on self-pity.

The shagbark reacted with a bumper crop.
Bombardiers flew them onto our deck.

Resentful, misunderstood,
unjustly embarrassed—I felt
human faults absolved nightly
in bed by the starry sky,
cell by cell
across sidereal space.

I climbed the peepal tree.

I had a mother and a father
one muttered, one shouted.
My mother, with an ironing board
sniped under her breath.

My eye healed but I saw
only a pixilated world,

each thing, a pincushion of points

every point broken
to infinity.

Music lessons

My brother and I hid
waiting for the other to grow up.
I in the pump room, confident about winning.
Upstairs the TV was on,
a day's homework, *Gulliver's Travels* (his)
Jane Austen (mine), dog-eared pages
we turn in order to live.

There he is at the piano, torturing keys
that he will abandon to play football.
No sound of my violin.
Neither was made for the concert stage.
Dismay. Unspoken shame.
Jibes and taunts as last lines
of a joke. Call from outdoor play.
Dogs' paws clicking the hardwood floor
where shoes weren't allowed.

The kitchen was a refectory.
Pots banged, a sink clogged with scrapings,
parsnips and carrots from soup
that fed the hungry house
with aromatic dill.
Time unreeled
emerged from its cataclysm
with us to stumble away
honor conventions (if dubious)
as though we agreed to their lives
in spite of visible lapses
recited with sarcasm
not meant for children.

Conventions ruled over family,

inaction touted values
immune to review, without choice,
no questions since opposition
displayed a form of stupidity
about which we were appalled.

Only after decades
when our pain was commonplace
is a world revoked, slowly,
imperceptively for us, so that now
any hope of this moment,
also imprints on it
the fact that we had no options.

We couldn't hear our own footsteps.

The artist

My pulse is strong, proud of it.
Beneath city cacophony,
lying beside my lover
drowsy pitch of desire.
Desire: Tarot's figure, Fool.

Phone messages partially deleted.
Bus tickets, plane reservations.
Hotels, villas, haciendas, towns on
no one's road map. Ones contemplated,
numbers left undialed,
scenes never begun, love unconsummated.
Repetition morphed into dull habit.

Did I wish it? Maybe. I felt art
has roots sunk in chaos,
the shock that one doesn't grow
from ether, that in letting go
imagination becomes its own truth.

Love journey scented jasmine—
these monuments the master
in singing school offers.
They guide me, seeming traditional.

The garden troll's catch: sweets everyday,
human contract with sorrow and joy—
imaginal mired in actual—
solace enough to shroud the faithless.

Translation: Let me be loved.

Landing

It was nearly climax
when I looked and saw sky
through trees, sickened
because of the colliery.
I woke my brother and said, '*What
has become of us*?' He rubbed
his eyes and said, pointing,
'*That fire is the sun
We're on* terra firma.'
And I said, '*The magnetism is strong.
We will never leave.*'

Working papers

Lesson of scenes omitting
any subject felt personal.
Dinner was to restrain chattering flatware
in spirit of repression.
A dispirited moral code.

Our rule to be silent was
exempt from mention of one's work.
I presumed it to teach us
means of polite discourse
to elevate feeding young animals

Also: to not speak in public
or inwardly to attribute to anyone
who did life as a narcissist,
a word, we believed, that was
a black spot, target of death.

If we spoke? If we became
mouthpiece of a point of view
uncomfortably our own?
Punishment would arrive
executioner never named.

It wasn't silence that we learned
(which has use in lives lived)
but voice of a compliant, caged inside,
a wild bird raging in captivity.

Outside voices mocked the ashy nest.
Injustice was our fiery heritage—
chains, cinders, weighing—
We knew in our bodies not to speak out

lest our secret transmutation
was then placed on balance pans.
By touch we knew one another,
an atmosphere we in tandem breathed.
At times it intoxicated, exultant.

Astonishing transcendent peace,
balm of seeing dawn again—
now in flightbones of old age—
with words for unreserved
expression, relief, bliss.

Even now as their expiration nears,
to have the pardon
for what it is, gift of wonder,
nothing to see.

Nothing.

Home

Frost. Rink of starlight
Frozen blades of grasses,
like nerve cells firing.
Moon rises for the skating party.
And the sun, lackluster impresario.
After which months defiantly passed
sowing dissent among us.
Lovers were exempted from themselves,
from the rest. Tending to desire, they
are not cut of cloth or cardboard.

We came from stars. You
are first to deny this. Restless
at home, you wish to travel
less in body, more in forethought,
in silence that is a fermenting.
Moods calculated in the equation.

In broad daylight, when we belong
to the world and its ministry,
stars hide in the moon's socket.
The kiss of lovers, a moonflower.

Our lawn turned rutted, stony
after reseeding in rainy season.
The drought didn't end.

But do traces persist, that
call to those who seek purity?
What of their reality?

Spring freed earth of malice,
our going under. Love:

image *sans* grounds—foreground,
background—of appeal.

Appeals court: no recourse.

Portrait of the heart

Slats of a jalousie,
slotted light. Street light
then moonlight, then dawn light.
An hour was impassable
but earth was coming round.
As a result each object gained a single face.

Digitalis in a Coke bottle.
Wind across the open mouth
a warning signal. In tempo
it grows undiminished, then minor
as though an ocean chewing at shore.

To view without dividers
frame window, village, planet
in one gaze, fuzzy at ridges
as focus is too weak
to hold centered.

Awareness that hours melted
not in the cauldron of becoming.
Things remain to cling, a word
stops forward movement.
Any word, *begin, begin.*
In imperative voice, blood pulses.

In systole thought congeals
a slanted light, stasis in feeling

a trace of origin
forbidden mercy.

Reality too true to copy,
exclamatory.

Then wind on foxglove dropping
their open-mouthed calyxes.

Chance

Constancy is aberration yet
a second comes to end each year.
Summer, winter, more so at dark solstice.
Backlighting brings out details
hid in spot where principles flourish.
We count on it, forget each second is
shorter than a noon shadow.
We celebrate a brandy toast,
until idiocy shocks us awake.

Practice lacks purpose. A need for order
not only our bodies' self-importance
but the feel of simple repetition
undoes a death wish.
The animal prefers doing things over.

When rime stops, what shows
doesn't negate or deny
the impression suspended, indifferent
to need and desire. Dark ecstasy.

In this longest night, we sit around
the fireplace. Outside the Milky Way
deepens to a fjord. Do we prepare future
or repair past? A choice
made by bloodline.

We amnesiacs, face backwards.

Epigenesis

On one end my brother, I
on the other of the row boat.
My father (I suppose) with the oars.
A lake like glass, surface glaring,
trees doubled at shore.
A rare family outing, binoculars,
a map, a travel book.
Our family prefers vicarious
to real experience.

There was music. He at the piano,
I, the viola. Always one ear cocked
for the timer. Relief and tears when done.
At least there were no drums
though making music seemed
an improbable route to fame.
We learned to bear ridicule.

There was conversation. Little.
Facts were reported, opinions
in brackets, by eyes, tone of voice.
Excessive thought while reading.
The dog scratched to be walked.

Our forbidden haven: the kitchen.
Smell of brisket, sighs
from my mother as she bent
to the oven door.

News of outside was less given
the more we knew. Divining,
deforming, disputing, all the while
we were insulated, immunized

against change by the daily round.
Little dramas as if scripted, letting
lives be what they were meant.

The script was holy, a version,
if altered; would incur punishment
any edit came across as heresy.

A force, terrifyingly strong
coursing through our bloodline.
which conserved smallest sins
of great-grandparents:
a full penitent inheritance
worth its weight in guilt.

Finally the present moment
encircles us like a dust devil
refusing form, cashing in ideals.
It bares an immediacy
a groundless hope.

Of consciousness.

The quilt

I wasn't ready. Earth, flowers and fruits.
You will learn to crave
seduction. It won't resist.

I sat with my mother, crocheting.
One square, then another. Colors mismatched,
skeins drooped on backs of chairs.
Each row added, the whole
grows incrementally. My brother
inveighs, each stitch in dispute.

Smell of new wool, from sheep
that crop our lawn, girding plum trees.
In picture frames, lace collars
matching faces that had tatted them.
My mother stretched smooth her portion
when it bunched. Deep contentment.
Absorption in work of making.
A refuge to escape life's hardness
asking nothing of will. It flowed.

Awakened tranquility,
click of the crochet hook
miming the pattern book's plan
binds you in comforting squares.
Outside the parlor, earth watched.

Soft pings on glass. I had
few provisions for winter.
The clicking had a hidden continuity.
Yet I had no power to break it,
deny myself rest. I tell you

what was never told me
in breach of love, sweet pain.

You will be unable to say no.
since release is forbidden.
Your body will become inert,
unable to enjoy animal life.

You and earth do not blend.
It cannot provide but for famine.

In other words, seduction will promise
but lack means—
you will remain without . . .

a hand reaches for grapes dangled.

By day

A word from our Latin book,
senex. The teacher said ageing.
We didn't, actually. We picked up speed,
to finish quicker.
Dying was when mass became light.

To pass through things or pass by.
If we stopped to feel it,
the secret was not brought to light.
That way, no attachments.
In a chase, there is no stop,
with our children, our lovers.
Although we were earnest,
they went lacking.

Dailiness was our assurance.
Clean, repair, undo, garden, house.
We tired of strange places.
We lived a convenience
that justified endless postponement.

Once we wanted little.
A false modesty to forestall praise,
a prayer for trifles. We kept watch
over ourselves, unweaving change by daylight.
It was never unfinished enough;
something was done, even
in face of our most stoic slogans.

It was not visible, harm
taking long silent walks
in the woods, 'guardians of nature,'

whispering among library stacks,
planting moss for rock gardens.

Life was normal as it was written,
controlled but an absence that
tailed us, its power was restraint
by insouciance. Our children took it
as religion and rebelled as believers.

When there was little to give,
the smallest seemed golden,
purple asters in autumn.
We said earth was poor
and helped ourselves to less than due.
Our children never grew up.

Or grew old, like a fragrance,
They subsisted, a scrum of brown dust:
proof that the world's poverty
could support only so much life,

a spore borne on wind's vagaries
as arid as the desert's.

Accumulation

The mirror looks back, marveling.
Four decades. Seen:
a self that refuses to be seen.
Your fingers clutch, sweaty
Eyes tear past image,
fearful of what might lie
in the tain, the burrowed brow.

Not familiar, which supposes contact,
but skirting in back of the face,
young still, brimmed with ambition
which means charisma

and so, a force that walls in,
displacing him from destination.
He isn't old but erased by years,
much to do, little to expect.

Others look different, they are.
at ease with people, happy at parties,
excited to impart secrets.

I often thought about that age,
coated with self-loathing,
doubts of friendship, respite granted
in supposing a future flawed
by a will to be known
but at a great distance
dilemma of the closed circuit.

Everything threatens to break in.

Intrigues that seek fantasy
amid the everyday.

That is to say, refusal of pure flux,
disquieting hungry ghosts.

I stood in the hearth's half-light,
reverie ended. At the mirror
my thoughts were suspended.
In the same breath, exaltation
blended with everyday dread.
Unmixed. Mixed. Seizing both.
I learned, came well-being,
what being human meant.

Before completion

When I paused to look
at the ribbon, light after dark,
encircling my vision, I caught one arm
of my brother. *Where are we going?*
His eyes saw it also; he said, *Home.*
I said, *then we're not yet finished.*